Given to:

With Love By:

© Copyright 2023 Joy Joyfully

Granddaughter
You are
LOVED!

Granddaughter,
you're so loved, it's true!
In every way, in all that you do.

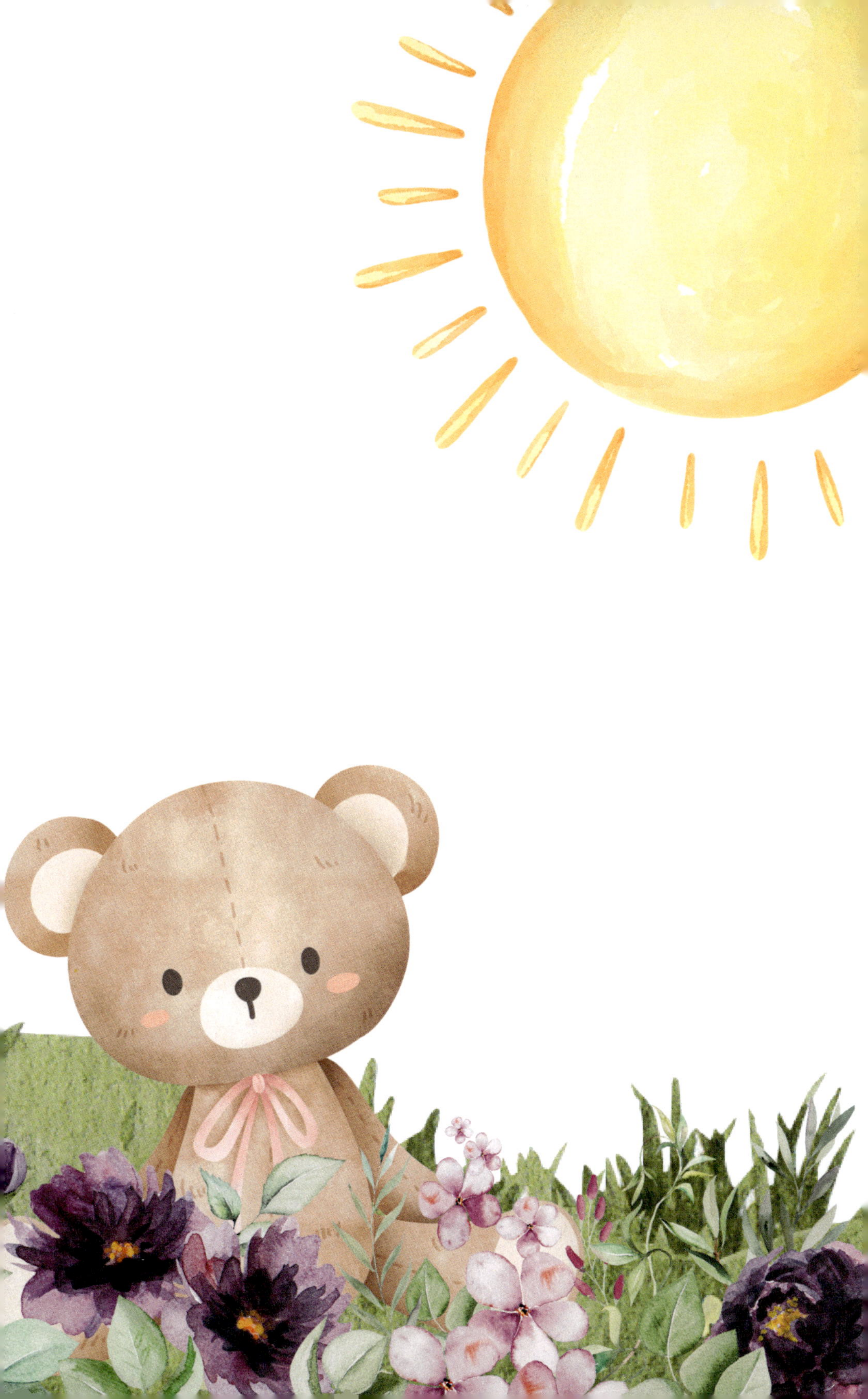

In a world where
kindness is sometimes rare,
Your compassion shines and glows,
it's beyond compare.

Donate

Your eyes are curious,
always seeking to find something new,
Each day is an exciting
adventure with you.

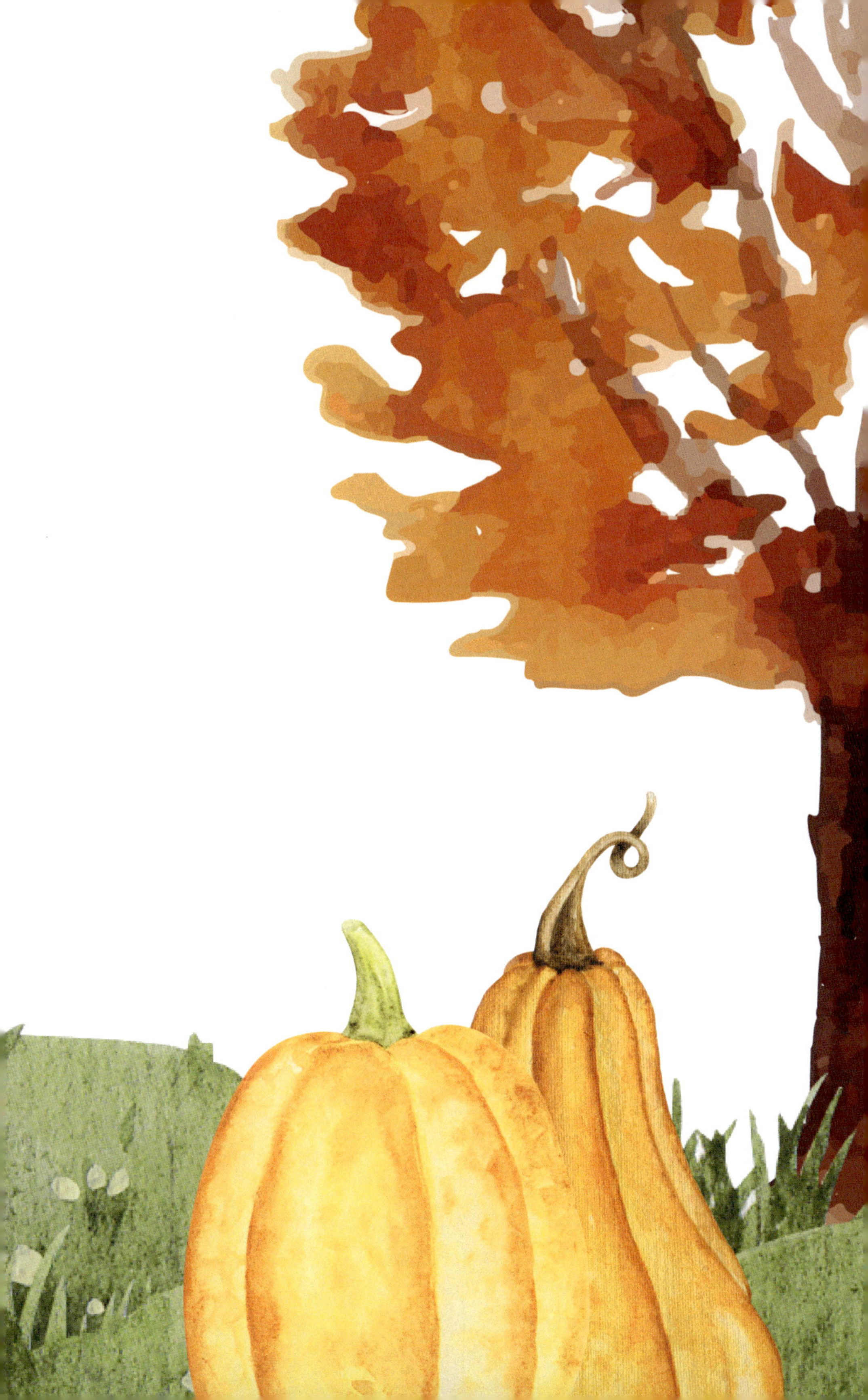

In the deep of winter,
You're like a warm sunray,
Spreading love like sunlight
on a cold snowy day.

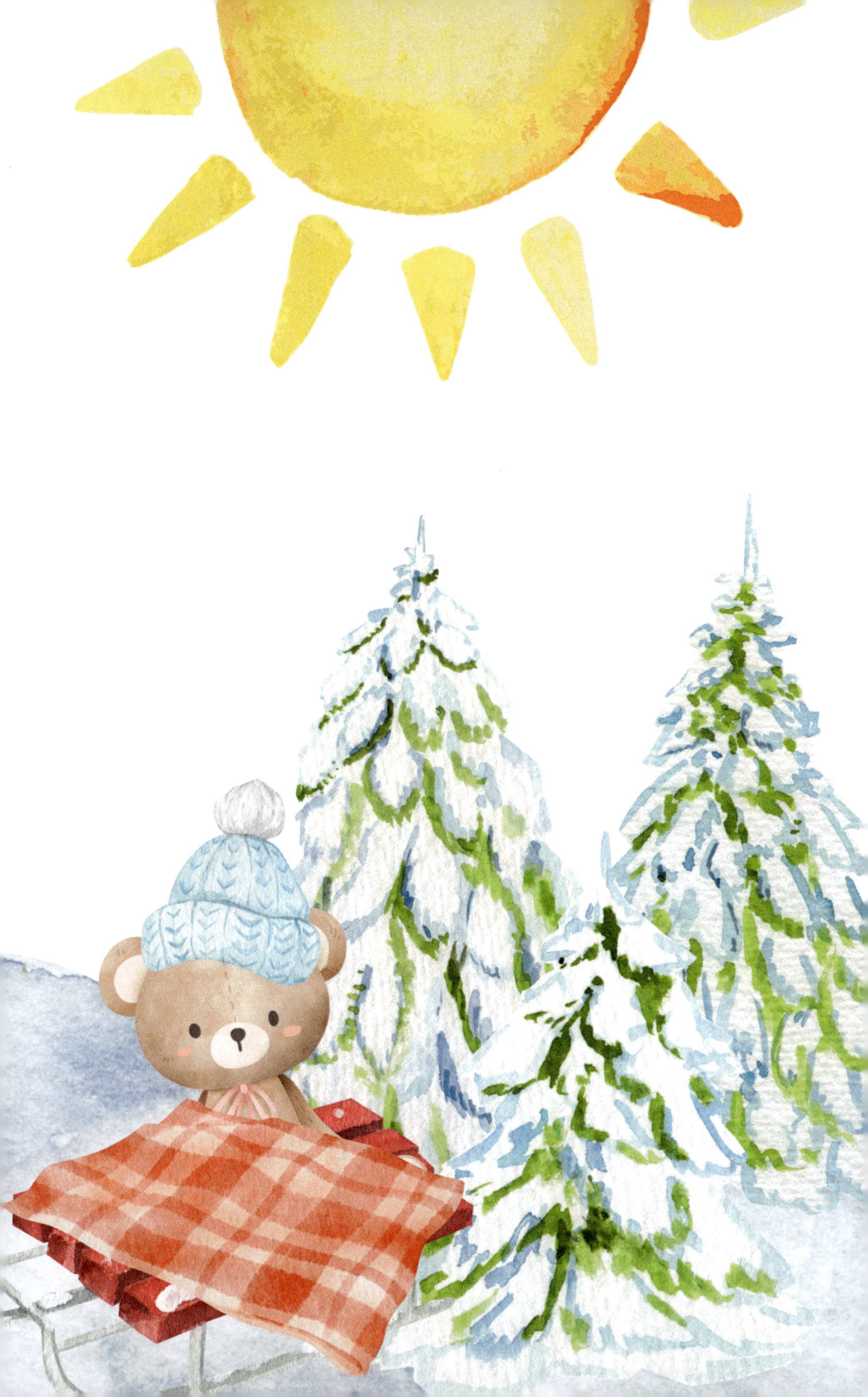

With a heart that's fair,
I know you'll stand strong,
Balancing truth and justice
when things go wrong.

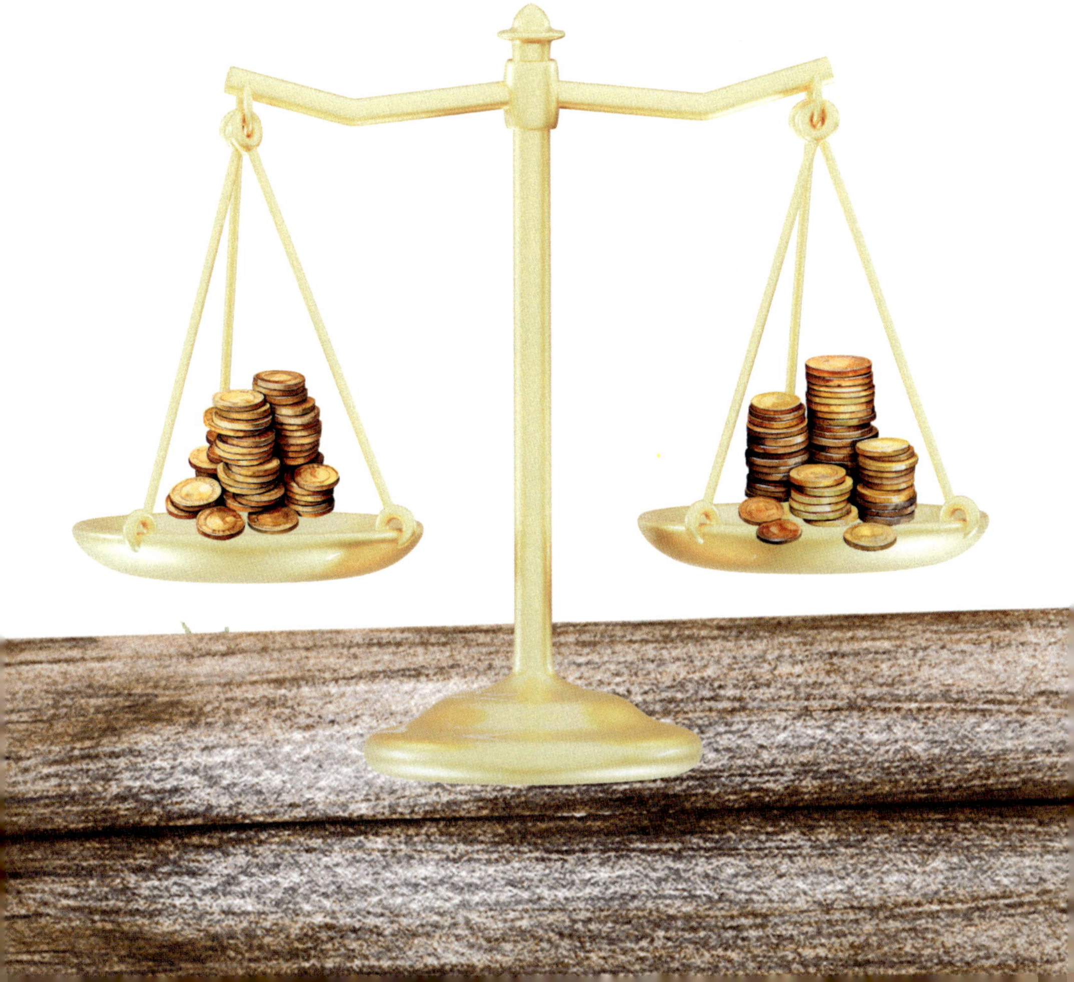

In your silliness,
a burst of joy takes flight,
When I'm laughing with you,
everything feels so right.

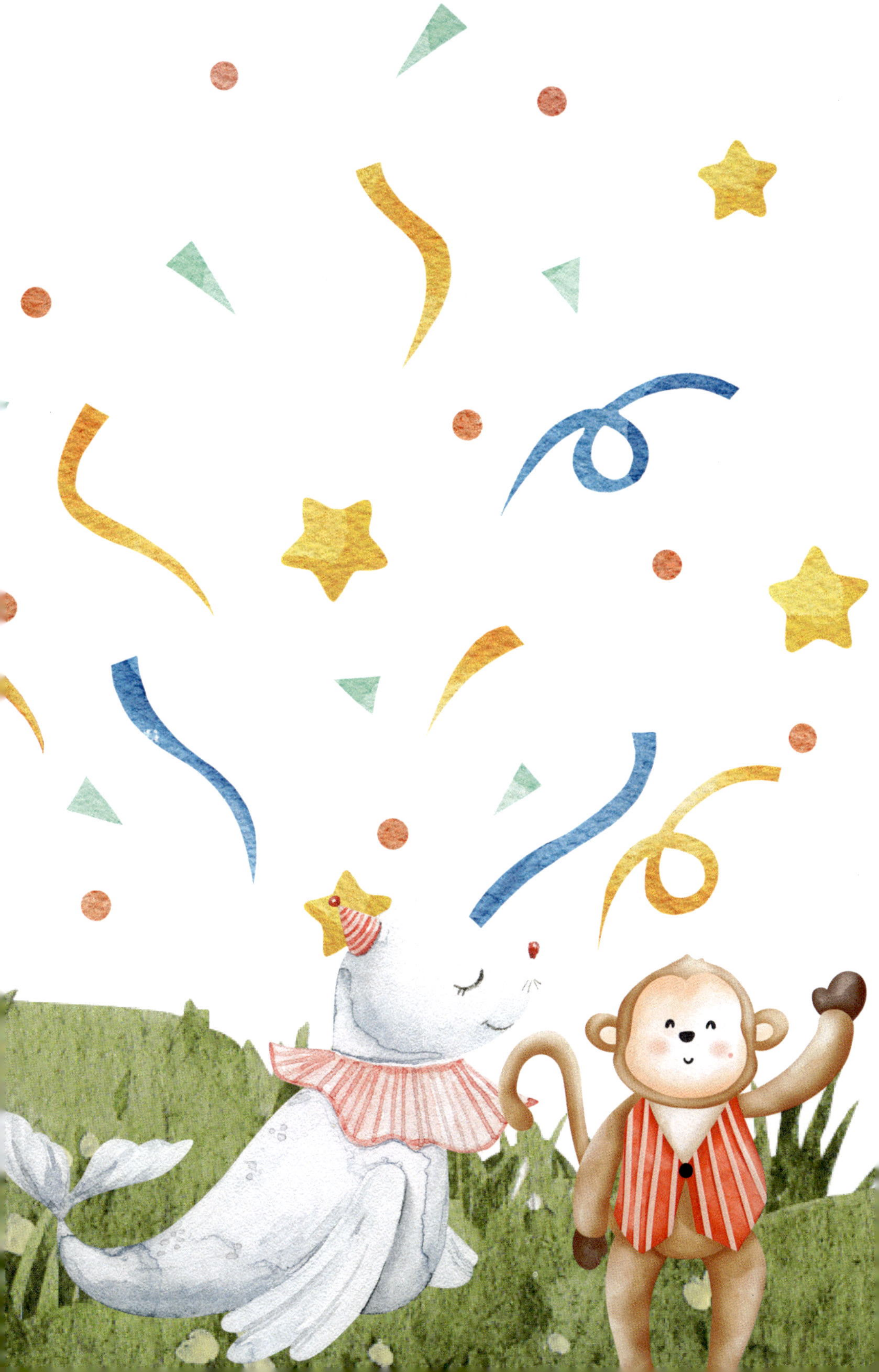

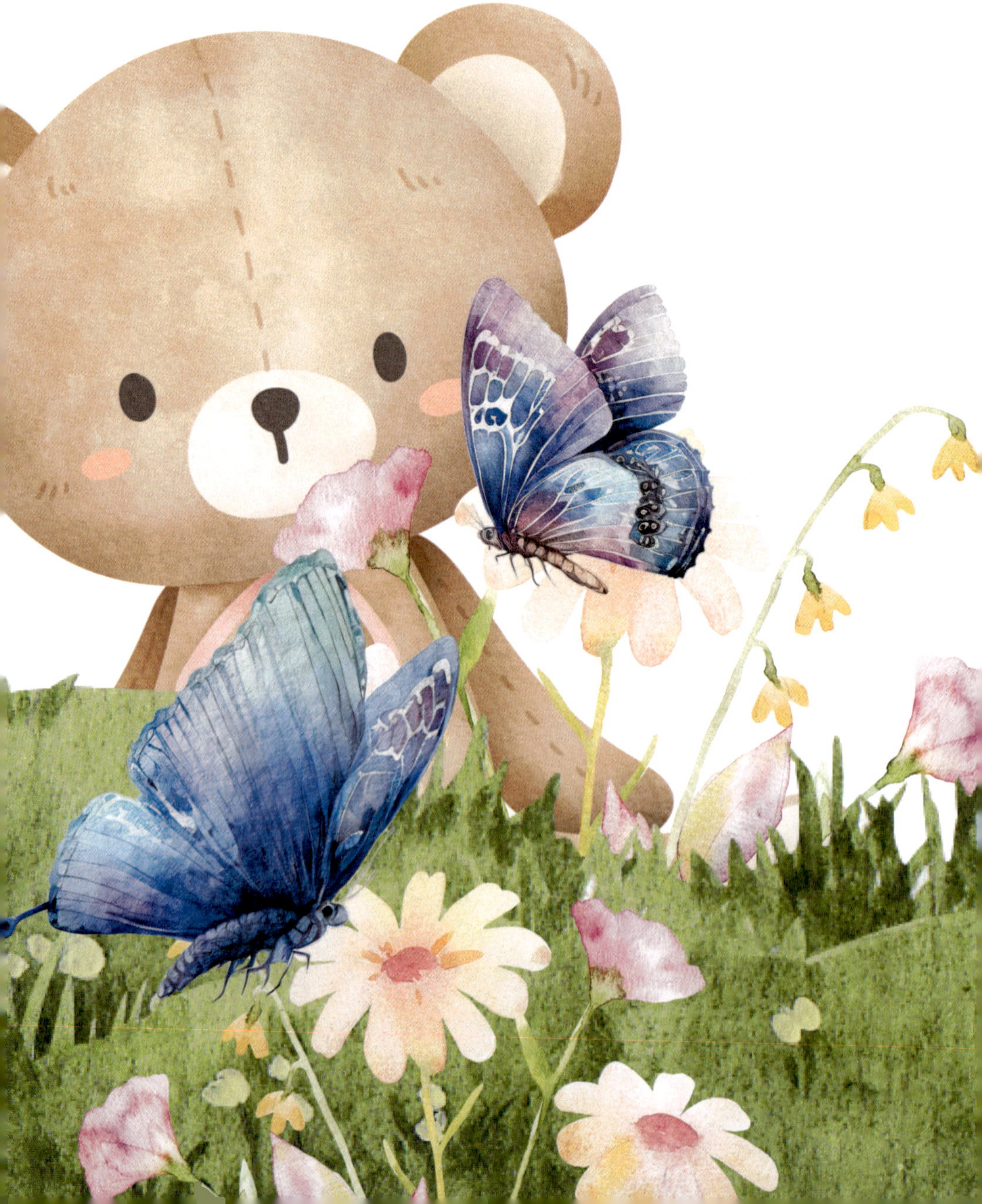

Granddaughter,

Your imagination is a wondrous place,
It is a big world of dreams,
Don't ever loose sight
of that joyful space.

When you are happy
or when you're feeling blue,
Remember,
Dear Granddaughter
My love for you will always
be true.

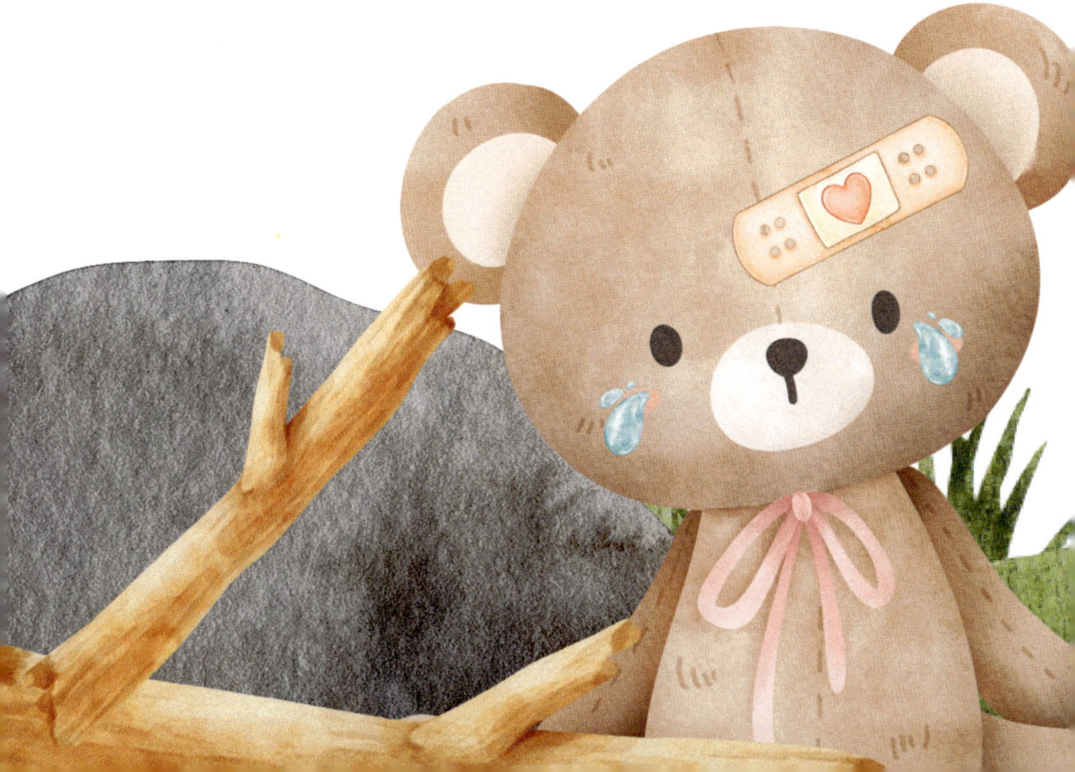

Whether close or far,
our love is like a song to play,
Dear Granddaughter,
our love will never fade away.

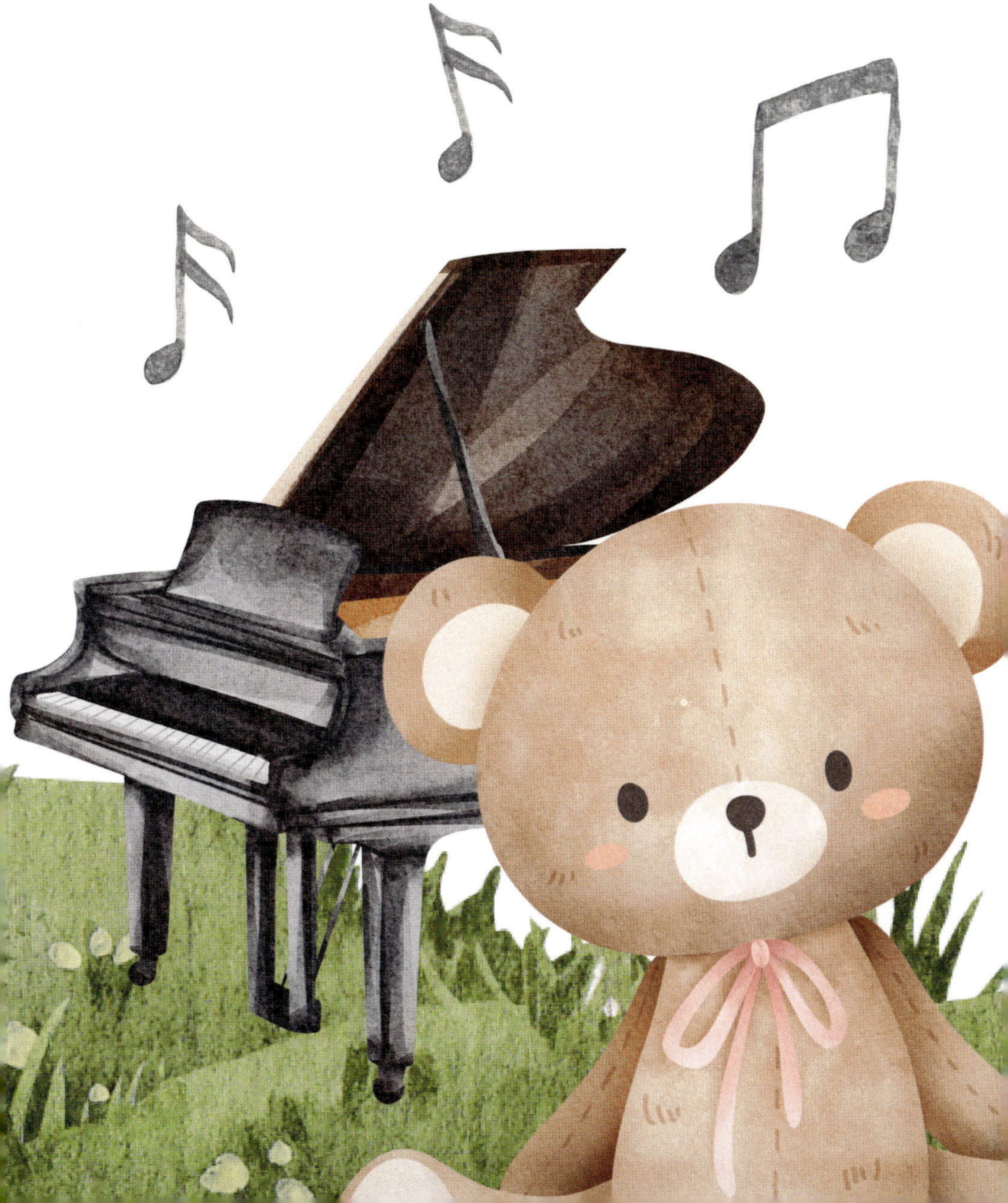

Granddaughter

You are adored,
in every smile and every tear,
You are treasured forever,
we will always hold you dear.

Granddaughter,

You are Loved!

The End

Made in the USA
Las Vegas, NV
17 March 2025